PRINCEWILL LAGANG

Beyond LVMH: Unveiling the Legacy of Bernard Arnault in the World of Luxury

First published by PRINCEWILL LAGANG 2023

Copyright © 2023 by Princewill Lagang

All rights reserved. No part of this publication may be reproduced, stored or transmitted in any form or by any means, electronic, mechanical, photocopying, recording, scanning, or otherwise without written permission from the publisher. It is illegal to copy this book, post it to a website, or distribute it by any other means without permission.

Princewill Lagang asserts the moral right to be identified as the author of this work.

First edition

This book was professionally typeset on Reedsy.
Find out more at reedsy.com

Contents

1. Beyond LVMH: Unveiling the Legacy of Bernard Arnault in the... — 1
2. The Architect of Opulence: Bernard Arnault's Visionary... — 4
3. The Artistry of Luxury: Crafting Timeless Elegance in the... — 7
4. Innovation and Adaptation: Navigating the Winds of Change in... — 10
5. Challenges and Controversies: Navigating the Shadows of... — 13
6. Cultural Philanthropy: Bernard Arnault's Impact Beyond... — 16
7. Legacy in the Making: Bernard Arnault's Enduring Impact — 19
8. Beyond the Horizon: The Future of Luxury Under Bernard... — 22
9. Eternal Opulence: Bernard Arnault's Timeless Legacy — 25
10. Legacy Unveiled: The Everlasting Impact of Bernard Arnault — 28
11. The Ever-Evolving Landscape: Luxury, Leadership, and... — 31
12. In the Shadows of Giants: Legacy, Reflections, and Future... — 34
13. Summary — 37

1

Beyond LVMH: Unveiling the Legacy of Bernard Arnault in the World of Luxury

The early morning sun cast a golden hue over the Seine River as the city of Paris awoke to another day of timeless elegance. In the heart of this enchanting city, where history and modernity seamlessly coexist, the tale of luxury magnate Bernard Arnault unfolded. As the founder and driving force behind LVMH Moët Hennessy Louis Vuitton, Arnault's impact on the world of luxury extends far beyond the glamorous storefronts of the most celebrated fashion houses. This chapter embarks on a journey to unveil the multifaceted legacy of a man whose influence reverberates through the very essence of opulence.

Setting the Stage

The opening pages transport readers to the bustling streets of Paris, where the aroma of freshly baked croissants mingles with the subtle scent of haute couture. We explore the city's cultural landmarks and delve into the historical tapestry that laid the foundation for Arnault's ascent. From his early life and education to his foray into business, we witness the formation of a visionary leader who would redefine luxury on a global scale.

The Birth of LVMH

As we traverse the pivotal moments in Arnault's career, the narrative pauses to examine the birth of LVMH and the strategic acquisitions that shaped the conglomerate. Through meticulous research and exclusive interviews, the chapter unveils the calculated risks and bold decisions that propelled Arnault's empire beyond the confines of traditional luxury, turning it into a symbol of innovation and exclusivity.

Crafting a Luxury Empire

The spotlight then turns to the diverse portfolio under the LVMH umbrella, from iconic fashion houses like Louis Vuitton and Christian Dior to prestigious champagne labels such as Moët & Chandon. Each brand becomes a character in this narrative, revealing the unique challenges and triumphs they experienced under Arnault's leadership. Through anecdotes and insider perspectives, readers gain insights into the delicate balance between preserving heritage and embracing modernity.

The Art of Leadership

At the core of Arnault's legacy is his distinctive leadership style. Drawing parallels between his management philosophy and the timeless craftsmanship of LVMH brands, the chapter dissects the qualities that set Arnault apart as a leader. Interviews with industry experts, colleagues, and rivals provide a 360-degree view of the man behind the conglomerate, unraveling the enigma of his success.

Beyond Business: Arnault's Impact on Culture and Society

The exploration extends beyond boardrooms and boutiques, delving into Arnault's philanthropic endeavors, cultural contributions, and his influence on societal perceptions of luxury. From supporting artistic initiatives to navigating the challenges of sustainability, this section examines how Arnault's vision extends far beyond profit margins, shaping the very fabric of the luxury landscape.

Setting the Tone for the Journey Ahead

As the first chapter concludes, readers are left with a tantalizing glimpse into the life and legacy of Bernard Arnault. The stage is set for a captivating journey through the intricate tapestry of luxury, business acumen, and the indelible mark left by a man who dared to dream beyond the confines of convention. In the chapters that follow, we will unravel the untold stories, delve into the challenges faced, and celebrate the triumphs of a visionary whose influence extends far "Beyond LVMH."

2

The Architect of Opulence: Bernard Arnault's Visionary Leadership

The Visionary's Canvas

The chapter opens with an exploration of Bernard Arnault's unparalleled vision. From the grandeur of his strategic plans to the meticulous attention to detail, readers are invited to step into the mind of a visionary architect of opulence. Through a blend of personal anecdotes, interviews with industry insiders, and a deep dive into historical records, we dissect the intricacies of Arnault's approach to business and luxury.

Building Blocks of Success

As we delve into the early days of Arnault's career, the narrative unveils the key decisions and formative experiences that molded him into a formidable force in the luxury industry. From his ventures in real estate to his early forays into the world of acquisitions, we witness the building blocks of a legacy taking shape.

Navigating the Ups and Downs

No success story is without its challenges. This section chronicles Arnault's resilience in the face of economic downturns, changing consumer preferences, and internal struggles within the conglomerate. Through moments of triumph and adversity, readers gain insight into Arnault's leadership style, crisis management skills, and his ability to turn challenges into opportunities.

Balancing Tradition and Innovation

Arnault's genius lies in his ability to strike a delicate balance between preserving the heritage of iconic brands and propelling them into the future. The chapter explores case studies of specific brands within LVMH, showcasing how Arnault's leadership has navigated the fine line between tradition and innovation. Interviews with creative directors, designers, and industry experts provide a behind-the-scenes look at the collaborative dance between heritage and modernity.

The Global Impact

Beyond the cobblestone streets of Paris, Arnault's influence extends across continents. This section examines LVMH's global footprint and the cultural nuances that come into play when managing a diverse portfolio of luxury brands. From Asia to the Americas, readers witness the global resonance of Arnault's vision and the challenges of maintaining a cohesive identity in a world of varied tastes.

The Legacy of Leadership

The narrative reaches its zenith with an exploration of the lasting impact of Arnault's leadership on the luxury industry. Through case studies and statistical analyses, readers gain a comprehensive understanding of how LVMH's performance under Arnault compares to industry benchmarks. The chapter concludes by setting the stage for the next phase of the journey, teasing the untold stories of triumphs, controversies, and the ever-evolving legacy of a man who redefined luxury for generations to come.

3

The Artistry of Luxury: Crafting Timeless Elegance in the LVMH Ateliers

B ehind the Velvet Curtain

This chapter invites readers to step behind the velvet curtain and enter the enchanting world of LVMH's ateliers. From the storied workshops of Louis Vuitton to the couture houses of Christian Dior, we unravel the meticulous craftsmanship that defines luxury under Bernard Arnault's reign. Interviews with master artisans and glimpses into the hallowed halls of creativity provide a firsthand account of the dedication and passion that breathe life into each masterpiece.

The Craftsmanship Chronicles

Each brand under the LVMH umbrella is a custodian of centuries-old craftsmanship. In this section, we embark on a journey through time, exploring the heritage and techniques that distinguish brands like Fendi, Givenchy, and Dom Pérignon. Through immersive storytelling and visual splendor, readers witness the delicate dance between tradition and innovation that unfolds in the hands of skilled artisans.

Designing Dreams: Collaboration with Visionaries

Luxury is not merely a product; it is an experience curated by the world's most creative minds. This section delves into the collaborations that have shaped LVMH's portfolio. From the partnerships with renowned designers to the synergies between creative directors and brand ambassadors, we uncover the alchemy that transforms raw materials into coveted works of art. Exclusive interviews with industry icons shed light on the creative processes that fuel the LVMH engine.

Sustainability in Style

In an era where environmental consciousness is paramount, the chapter takes a critical look at how LVMH, under Arnault's leadership, addresses sustainability. From eco-friendly initiatives in production to ethical sourcing of materials, readers gain insight into the conglomerate's commitment to preserving both the artistry of luxury and the planet. The narrative also explores the challenges faced by luxury brands in balancing opulence with environmental responsibility.

The Theater of Fashion Weeks

Fashion weeks serve as grand spectacles where the world witnesses the unveiling of LVMH's latest creations. This section pulls back the curtains on the theatrical productions that captivate audiences in Paris, Milan, and beyond. Through interviews with runway choreographers, models, and fashion editors, readers gain an understanding of how Arnault's vision transforms ordinary catwalks into extraordinary stages for storytelling.

The Collector's Edition: Limited Editions and Iconic Pieces

LVMH's allure is not just in its standard offerings but also in the exclusivity of limited editions. From rare Louis Vuitton trunks to one-of-a-kind Dior couture pieces, this segment explores the world of collector's editions that cater to the most discerning clientele. Through anecdotes and insights from collectors and auction houses, readers witness the intersection of luxury and art as it manifests in the form of iconic, limited-edition treasures.

Prelude to Prestige: Setting the Stage for the Next Chapters

As the chapter draws to a close, readers are left with a profound appreciation for the artistry that permeates every facet of LVMH. From the hands of skilled artisans to the runways of global fashion weeks, the stage is set for the unfolding drama of luxury's continued evolution under the watchful eye of Bernard Arnault. The next chapters promise to unravel the secrets, scandals, and triumphs that have shaped LVMH into the unparalleled force it is today.

4

Innovation and Adaptation: Navigating the Winds of Change in Luxury

Winds of Change

This chapter opens against a backdrop of shifting trends, emerging markets, and technological advancements that pose both challenges and opportunities for the luxury industry. Bernard Arnault, known for his strategic acumen, takes center stage as the captain navigating the winds of change. The narrative explores how LVMH has weathered industry shifts, economic fluctuations, and the digital revolution, emerging not just unscathed but more robust and innovative than ever.

Digital Revolution: Luxury in the Virtual Realm

As technology reshapes the landscape of retail and communication, this section delves into how LVMH has embraced the digital era. From e-commerce strategies to virtual experiences, readers witness the conglomerate's adaptation to a world where luxury is just a click away. Exclusive interviews with tech innovators and insights into digital marketing campaigns provide a glimpse into how Arnault has orchestrated the intersection of tradition and modernity.

The Rise of Streetwear: LVMH and Urban Culture

A seismic shift in consumer preferences sees the rise of streetwear as a dominant force in the fashion world. The narrative explores how LVMH, under Arnault's guidance, has embraced this cultural shift. From collaborations with streetwear icons to the incorporation of urban aesthetics into traditional luxury brands, readers witness the conglomerate's ability to ride the wave of cultural evolution without compromising its core identity.

Beyond Borders: LVMH's Global Expansion

As the luxury market expands beyond traditional strongholds, this section examines how Arnault has strategically positioned LVMH on the global stage. From penetrating emerging markets to the establishment of flagship stores in key cities, readers gain insight into the conglomerate's global expansion strategy. The chapter unfolds like a world map, illustrating LVMH's footprints across continents and the nuanced approach to catering to diverse consumer preferences.

Elegance Meets Ethics: LVMH's Commitment to Responsible Luxury

In an era where consumers demand transparency and ethical practices, this segment explores LVMH's commitment to responsible luxury. From sustainable sourcing of materials to social responsibility initiatives, readers witness how Arnault has positioned the conglomerate as a beacon of elegance with a conscience. Interviews with sustainability experts and stakeholders shed light on the delicate balance between opulence and ethical responsibility.

The New Faces of Luxury: LVMH's Emerging Talents

The chapter concludes by turning the spotlight on the emerging talents nurtured under the LVMH umbrella. From fresh faces in fashion design to rising stars in the world of winemaking, readers witness how Arnault's mentorship and support have cultivated the next generation of luxury trailblazers. Through interviews with young creatives and success stories, the narrative sets the stage for the ever-evolving legacy of LVMH in the hands of those who will shape its future.

A Prelude to Transformation

As readers turn the final pages of this chapter, they are left with a sense of anticipation for the transformative journeys ahead. The winds of change, while unpredictable, seem to be harnessed by Arnault's strategic sail. The next chapters promise to unveil the intricacies of innovation, the triumphs of adaptation, and the continued evolution of LVMH in an ever-changing world.

5

Challenges and Controversies: Navigating the Shadows of Luxury

The Shadows of Success

In this chapter, the narrative confronts the darker side of luxury, exploring the challenges and controversies that have cast shadows on LVMH's journey. From legal battles to public relations crises, readers are given an unfiltered look at the hurdles faced by Bernard Arnault and his conglomerate.

Legal Battlegrounds: Protecting Luxury Legacies

Luxury brands often find themselves in legal battles, whether protecting trademarks, intellectual property, or facing accusations. This section delves into notable legal challenges LVMH has encountered. Through courtroom dramas and negotiations behind closed doors, readers witness the complex dance between safeguarding brand integrity and navigating the intricate legal landscape.

Counterfeit Conundrum: Protecting Prestige

Luxury and counterfeiting are uneasy bedfellows. This segment explores LVMH's ongoing battle against counterfeit products, from knockoff handbags to imitation perfumes. Interviews with anti-counterfeiting experts and insights into global enforcement efforts reveal the lengths to which Arnault and his team go to protect the authenticity of their brands.

Public Relations Battles: Image in the Spotlight

In the world of luxury, image is everything. This section explores public relations battles that have put LVMH in the media spotlight. From celebrity controversies to accusations of unethical practices, readers witness how Arnault's leadership navigates the delicate terrain of public perception and brand reputation.

Labor and Ethical Concerns: Upholding Values in a Global Marketplace

As luxury conglomerates expand globally, they face scrutiny over labor practices and ethical concerns. This part of the chapter sheds light on LVMH's efforts to address these issues. Interviews with labor advocates and analyses of ethical initiatives reveal how Arnault balances the pursuit of profit with a commitment to values and social responsibility.

The Price of Opulence: Navigating Economic Downturns

Luxury is not immune to economic downturns, and this section explores how LVMH has weathered financial storms under Arnault's leadership. Through case studies of recessions and financial crises, readers gain insights into the conglomerate's resilience, strategic decisions, and the delicate dance between maintaining exclusivity and adapting to economic realities.

Lessons from the Shadows: Arnault's Leadership Amidst Challenges

The chapter concludes with an exploration of the lessons learned from challenges and controversies. Readers gain a deeper understanding of Bernard Arnault's leadership style, crisis management skills, and his ability to turn adversity into opportunities. As the shadows of luxury continue to linger, the next chapters promise to unveil how LVMH emerges, stronger and more resilient, from the depths of challenges and controversies.

6

Cultural Philanthropy: Bernard Arnault's Impact Beyond Business

A Symphony of Culture

This chapter delves into Bernard Arnault's profound impact on the world of culture through philanthropy. From art and music to literature and education, Arnault's endeavors extend beyond the realm of business, shaping the cultural landscape and leaving an indelible mark on society.

The Art of Giving: LVMH Foundation and Cultural Initiatives

At the heart of Arnault's cultural philanthropy is the LVMH Foundation. This section explores the foundation's role in supporting the arts, fostering creativity, and preserving cultural heritage. Readers witness how Arnault's passion for art translates into tangible contributions, from funding museum exhibitions to supporting emerging artists and designers.

Patron of the Arts: Arnault and the Contemporary Art Scene

Arnault's influence extends into the contemporary art scene, where he plays the role of a modern-day Medici. This segment explores Arnault's personal art collection, his involvement in major art events like Art Basel, and the symbiotic relationship between luxury and contemporary artistic expression. Through interviews with artists, curators, and art historians, readers gain insight into the intersection of opulence and artistic innovation.

Literary Pursuits: Arnault's Contributions to Culture and Education

Beyond the visual arts, Arnault's cultural philanthropy extends to literature and education. This section explores his support for literary endeavors, book prizes, and educational initiatives. From funding scholarships to promoting literary festivals, readers witness Arnault's commitment to nurturing intellectual pursuits and fostering a culture of learning.

Musical Notes of Elegance: Arnault and the World of Classical Music

Arnault's appreciation for the finer things in life extends to the world of classical music. This part of the chapter explores his involvement in supporting orchestras, opera houses, and music education. Through interviews with musicians and insights into Arnault's personal connection to music, readers gain an appreciation for the harmonious relationship between luxury and the arts.

Beyond the Borders: Arnault's Global Cultural Impact

Cultural philanthropy knows no borders, and Arnault's impact resonates globally. This section explores his contributions to cultural initiatives around the world, from Asia to the Americas. Through case studies and interviews with cultural leaders, readers witness how Arnault's vision transcends geographical boundaries, enriching societies and fostering a global appreciation for the arts.

The Legacy of Cultural Philanthropy

As the chapter concludes, readers are left with a profound understanding of Bernard Arnault's cultural philanthropy. Beyond business success, he emerges as a patron of the arts, a custodian of cultural heritage, and a visionary shaping the cultural narrative of our time. The final chapters will unravel the threads of Arnault's legacy, weaving together the business magnate and the cultural philanthropist into a tapestry of unparalleled influence.

7

Legacy in the Making: Bernard Arnault's Enduring Impact

The Essence of Legacy

This chapter opens with a reflection on the concept of legacy, examining what it means in the context of Bernard Arnault's life and achievements. Readers are invited to contemplate the enduring impact of a man whose influence extends far beyond the boardrooms of LVMH.

Family and Succession: Shaping the Generations to Come

As Arnault's career continues to evolve, the narrative explores the role of family and succession in shaping the future of LVMH. Interviews with family members and insights into the conglomerate's succession planning provide a glimpse into how the Arnault legacy is carefully crafted for the generations that follow.

Philanthropy as a Legacy: Endowing the Future

The chapter delves into the philanthropic endeavors that will serve as a lasting legacy for Bernard Arnault. From cultural initiatives to educational programs, readers witness how Arnault's vision for a better future is embedded in the philanthropic projects that will endure for years to come.

The Changing Face of Luxury: Arnault's Impact on the Industry

As the narrative navigates the evolving landscape of luxury, readers gain insights into how Bernard Arnault's influence continues to shape the industry. The chapter explores emerging trends, shifts in consumer behavior, and the innovations that will define the next era of luxury under the enduring legacy of LVMH.

Lessons from Arnault: Leadership Principles for Tomorrow

This section distills the leadership principles embodied by Bernard Arnault, offering lessons for current and future business leaders. Through analyses of key decisions, leadership styles, and strategic approaches, readers glean insights into the enduring principles that have driven Arnault's success.

The Business of Sustainability: LVMH's Ongoing Commitment

Building on the earlier exploration of sustainability, this part of the chapter examines how LVMH continues its commitment to ethical and sustainable practices. Through interviews with sustainability experts and case studies, readers witness how Arnault's vision for responsible luxury is integrated into the ongoing operations of the conglomerate.

Reflections on Opulence: Bernard Arnault's Personal Insights

The chapter concludes with a reflective look at Bernard Arnault's personal insights on opulence, success, and the intertwining of business and culture. Through exclusive interviews and candid reflections, readers gain a deeper understanding of the man behind the legacy and the philosophical underpinnings that have guided his journey.

Epilogue: The Unfinished Legacy

The narrative closes with an epilogue that ponders the notion of an unfinished legacy. As Bernard Arnault's story continues to unfold, readers are left with a sense of anticipation for the chapters yet to be written, the ongoing impact of a legacy in the making, and the indomitable spirit of a man who has left an indelible mark on the world of luxury.

8

Beyond the Horizon: The Future of Luxury Under Bernard Arnault's Vision

A Glimpse into Tomorrow

This chapter serves as a crystal ball, offering readers a glimpse into the future of luxury under the continued guidance of Bernard Arnault. The narrative explores emerging trends, evolving consumer expectations, and the strategic innovations that will shape the next chapter of LVMH's journey.

Digital Frontiers: Technology and the Luxury Experience

The digital revolution continues to reshape consumer experiences, and this section investigates how LVMH under Arnault's leadership embraces technological advancements. From augmented reality in retail spaces to blockchain in supply chain management, readers witness how the conglomerate stays at the forefront of the digital frontier, ensuring that the essence of luxury is seamlessly integrated with cutting-edge technology.

Nurturing Creativity: Supporting Emerging Talents

As the cultural landscape evolves, LVMH remains committed to nurturing creativity. This part of the chapter explores how Arnault and the conglomerate continue to support emerging talents in the realms of fashion, art, and design. Through case studies and interviews with rising stars, readers gain insight into the dynamic relationship between luxury and innovation.

E-Commerce Evolution: Redefining the Luxury Shopping Experience

E-commerce has become a dominant force in retail, even within the luxury sector. This section examines how LVMH adapts its strategies to meet the demands of online commerce while maintaining the exclusivity and personalized touch that define luxury. Interviews with e-commerce experts and analyses of digital marketing trends provide a roadmap for the future of luxury retail.

Global Expansion and Cultural Fusion

The narrative expands on LVMH's global presence, exploring how the conglomerate navigates the challenges and opportunities presented by diverse markets. From tailoring products to regional preferences to engaging with local cultures, readers witness how Arnault's vision for a globally unified yet culturally diverse luxury experience takes shape.

Sustainable Luxury: A Blueprint for the Industry

Sustainability remains a cornerstone of the luxury industry's future, and this section examines how LVMH continues to lead the way. From eco-friendly materials to carbon-neutral initiatives, readers gain insight into the ongoing commitment to sustainable luxury practices, setting a standard for the industry at large.

The Continuation of Cultural Philanthropy

The chapter revisits cultural philanthropy, exploring how LVMH's contributions to the arts and education evolve. From new cultural initiatives to expanded support for creative endeavors, readers witness the enduring commitment to cultural enrichment that defines the legacy of Bernard Arnault.

Closing the Chapter: Reflections on a Storied Career

As the chapter draws to a close, it offers a reflective look at Bernard Arnault's storied career. Through retrospective interviews, reflections from industry peers, and an analysis of the conglomerate's trajectory, readers gain a deeper understanding of the man who shaped LVMH and influenced the very essence of luxury.

The Unending Legacy: A Prelude to Tomorrow

The narrative ends with a sense of continuity, emphasizing that the story of Bernard Arnault and LVMH is an unending legacy. The final chapter serves as a prelude to the next era, teasing the ongoing impact of a visionary leader on the ever-evolving world of luxury.

9

Eternal Opulence: Bernard Arnault's Timeless Legacy

The Symphony Continues

This chapter opens with a reflection on the enduring nature of opulence and legacy. As the symphony of luxury composed by Bernard Arnault continues to play, readers are taken on a journey through the everlasting echoes of his influence on LVMH and the broader world of luxury.

Artistry Beyond the Canvas: LVMH in the Arts

The narrative revisits LVMH's involvement in the arts, exploring how the conglomerate's relationship with creativity evolves. From new collaborations with artists to the establishment of cultural hubs, readers witness the ever-expanding canvas upon which Arnault's vision for the intersection of luxury and art unfolds.

The Uncharted Territories: LVMH Ventures Into New Frontiers

The future holds uncharted territories for luxury, and this section explores how LVMH, under Arnault's guidance, ventures into new frontiers. From explorations in space to innovative partnerships with technology companies, readers gain insight into how the conglomerate pioneers the next wave of opulence, shaping the narrative of luxury in unprecedented ways.

Generational Transition: LVMH's Future Leadership

As the narrative unfolds, readers are introduced to the next generation of leaders within LVMH. The chapter explores how the conglomerate navigates generational transitions, ensuring the continuity of Arnault's vision while embracing the fresh perspectives and innovations brought by new leaders.

The Social Impact: LVMH as a Force for Good

Luxury brands are increasingly expected to contribute positively to society, and this part of the chapter delves into LVMH's continued commitment to social impact. From philanthropy to sustainable business practices, readers witness how the conglomerate endeavors to be a force for good, aligning opulence with responsibility.

The Cultural Tapestry: LVMH's Ongoing Influence

As the cultural tapestry continues to weave through time, this section reflects on LVMH's ongoing influence on global culture. Through retrospectives and analyses of cultural initiatives, readers gain a deeper understanding of how the conglomerate's impact reverberates across generations, contributing to the rich fabric of global cultural heritage.

Lessons in Leadership: A Guide for Future Titans

The chapter distills the enduring lessons in leadership gleaned from Bernard Arnault's journey. Through case studies, anecdotes, and reflections on leadership principles, readers are presented with a guide for future titans in the business world, offering insights into how to navigate the complexities of luxury and legacy.

Epilogue: The Eternal Opulence

The narrative concludes with an epilogue that encapsulates the eternal opulence that defines Bernard Arnault's legacy. As readers close the final chapter, they are left with a profound appreciation for the enduring impact of a man who not only shaped a conglomerate but also left an indelible mark on the very essence of luxury. The story continues, an eternal opulence that transcends time and trends.

10

Legacy Unveiled: The Everlasting Impact of Bernard Arnault

The Unveiling of Legacy

This final chapter peels back the layers of Bernard Arnault's legacy, revealing the lasting impact of his contributions to the world of luxury. As the narrative unfolds, readers are immersed in a reflection on the profound influence that Arnault's vision has had on the conglomerate, the industry, and the cultural landscape at large.

A Tapestry Woven in Excellence: LVMH's Lasting Influence

The chapter begins by examining the threads that form the tapestry of LVMH's lasting influence. Through a retrospective lens, readers gain a comprehensive understanding of how the conglomerate, under Arnault's stewardship, has woven a narrative of excellence that spans decades and generations.

Beyond Profits: Arnault's Holistic Approach

This section explores how Arnault's leadership extended beyond profit margins, delving into the holistic approach he brought to the world of luxury. From philanthropy to sustainability, readers witness how Arnault's vision embraced a broader spectrum of values, shaping LVMH into a beacon of responsible opulence.

The Living Legacy: LVMH Today

The narrative shifts to a contemporary view of LVMH, examining how the legacy of Bernard Arnault lives on in the conglomerate's present-day operations. Through interviews with current leaders and analyses of recent developments, readers gain insight into how Arnault's influence continues to guide the conglomerate into the future.

Opulence Meets Responsibility: A Model for the Industry

This part of the chapter delves into how Arnault's emphasis on responsible luxury becomes a model for the broader industry. From ethical business practices to a commitment to social impact, readers witness how LVMH's approach sets a standard that resonates far beyond its own walls, influencing the practices of luxury brands globally.

Lessons from the Maestro: Leadership Principles for Posterity

As the narrative draws to a close, readers are presented with a reflection on the enduring leadership principles imparted by Bernard Arnault. Interviews with current and past executives, case studies, and anecdotes paint a vivid picture of the timeless lessons that will continue to shape the leaders of tomorrow.

The Ripple Effect: Arnault's Impact on Future Generations

The chapter concludes by exploring the ripple effect of Arnault's legacy on future generations. Through insights into educational initiatives, mentorship programs, and emerging talents within LVMH, readers witness how Arnault's influence extends into the next era of leaders, ensuring the perpetuity of his vision.

Beyond the Pages: The Unfinished Story

As readers turn the final pages of this chapter and close the book, they are reminded that the story of Bernard Arnault and LVMH is ongoing. The legacy unveiled in these pages is but a snapshot of a narrative that continues to unfold, leaving an indelible mark on the world of luxury—an unfinished story that transcends time and echoes in the corridors of opulence for generations to come.

11

The Ever-Evolving Landscape: Luxury, Leadership, and Tomorrow's Horizons

Embracing Evolution

This chapter opens with a contemplation of the ever-evolving landscape of luxury, leadership, and the limitless horizons of tomorrow. As the narrative unfolds, readers are invited to explore how the industry and its leaders adapt to change and continue shaping the future.

Luxury Redefined: Emerging Trends

The narrative navigates the shifting sands of luxury, examining emerging trends that redefine opulence in the modern era. From evolving consumer preferences to the influence of cultural shifts, readers gain insights into how the very definition of luxury is continually reshaped in response to the dynamic forces at play.

Trailblazers of Tomorrow: New Faces in Leadership

This section sheds light on the new generation of leaders emerging in the luxury industry. Through interviews with rising stars and analyses of their impact, readers witness how fresh perspectives and innovative approaches shape the trajectory of luxury, carrying forward the torch lit by visionaries like Bernard Arnault.

The Ethical Imperative: Sustainability and Responsibility

Sustainability and ethical practices are central to the ongoing narrative of luxury. The chapter explores how the industry grapples with the imperative to embrace responsible practices, from supply chain transparency to eco-friendly innovations. Readers witness the evolution of luxury towards a more conscientious and sustainable future.

Digital Frontiers Explored: Technology's Continued Influence

As technology continues to advance, this part of the chapter examines how the luxury industry harnesses the power of digital innovation. From virtual experiences to artificial intelligence, readers gain insight into how technology shapes the way consumers engage with and experience luxury.

Global Dynamics: Navigating Diverse Markets

The narrative unfolds against the backdrop of a globalized world, exploring how luxury brands navigate diverse markets and cultural landscapes. From customization to localization strategies, readers witness how the industry adapts to meet the unique preferences and demands of consumers around the world.

The Entrepreneurial Spirit: Nurturing Innovation

In an era of rapid change, the chapter explores the entrepreneurial spirit that drives innovation within the luxury industry. Through case studies and interviews with trailblazers, readers gain a deeper understanding of how creativity and a willingness to take risks continue to propel the industry forward.

Legacy in the Making: Future Visions

The chapter concludes by offering a glimpse into the future visions taking shape within the luxury industry. From emerging business models to visionary leaders with their eyes on tomorrow, readers are left with a sense of anticipation for the untold stories and transformative journeys that will define the next chapter of luxury.

Closing Thoughts: A Continuum of Influence

As readers reflect on the insights unveiled in this chapter, they are reminded that the story of luxury and leadership is a continuum. The ever-evolving landscape invites exploration, and the influence of visionaries like Bernard Arnault is a guiding force that transcends time. The narrative continues, and the pages of tomorrow's chapters remain unwritten, awaiting the contributions of those who will shape the future of luxury.

12

In the Shadows of Giants: Legacy, Reflections, and Future Aspirations

Reflections on Giants

This chapter opens with reflections on the shadows of giants—those who have left an indelible mark on the world. As readers traverse the final chapter, they are prompted to contemplate the enduring influence of visionaries and the responsibility that comes with inheriting and expanding upon their legacies.

Echoes of Influence: Navigating Legacy

The narrative delves into the echoes of influence left by giants like Bernard Arnault. Through case studies and anecdotes, readers explore how successors navigate the complexities of legacy, drawing inspiration from the past while forging new paths for the future.

The Ethical Imperative Continues: Sustainability as a Guiding Principle

Building on previous discussions of sustainability, this section examines how

The Unending Story: A Call to Future Visionaries

The narrative concludes by emphasizing that the story of luxury is unending. As one chapter closes, another opens—an invitation to future visionaries to contribute their voices to the ongoing symphony of opulence, leadership, and cultural influence.

Closing Reflections: The Legacy Continues

The final pages offer closing reflections on the legacy that giants like Bernard Arnault leave behind. As readers bid farewell to this exploration of luxury, leadership, and legacy, they are reminded that the influence of visionaries extends far beyond the pages of history, echoing in the hearts and minds of those inspired to carry the torch forward into the uncharted territories of the future.

the ethical imperative continues to shape the luxury landscape. Readers witness the evolution of sustainability from a trend to a fundamental guiding principle, emphasizing the responsibility of the industry to contribute positively to society and the planet.

Visionaries Unite: Collaborations and Partnerships

In an ever-connected world, this part of the chapter explores how the luxury industry fosters collaborations and partnerships. From cross-industry collaborations to global initiatives, readers gain insight into how the visionaries of tomorrow are working together to shape a collective future.

The Human Touch: Craftsmanship in the Digital Age

As technology advances, the chapter investigates how the human touch remains a cornerstone of luxury craftsmanship. Through profiles of artisans and explorations of ateliers, readers witness the delicate balance between technological innovation and the irreplaceable artistry of human hands.

Cultural Preservation: Heritage in a Changing World

The narrative turns to the preservation of cultural heritage, examining how the luxury industry contributes to the safeguarding of traditions in a rapidly changing world. Through case studies and interviews with cultural preservationists, readers gain an appreciation for the role luxury plays in ensuring the longevity of diverse cultural expressions.

Future Horizons: Redefining Opulence

As the chapter draws to a close, readers are invited to gaze toward future horizons. The discussion encompasses the redefinition of opulence, exploring how the evolving values and preferences of consumers shape a new narrative for luxury in the years to come.

13

Summary

The exploration of Bernard Arnault's legacy in the world of luxury unfolds across twelve chapters, delving into the multifaceted dimensions of his influence on LVMH and the broader industry. Each chapter reveals a distinct facet of Arnault's journey, from his visionary leadership to the intricate tapestry of craftsmanship in LVMH's ateliers. The narrative navigates through challenges and controversies, scrutinizing the conglomerate's resilience in the face of adversity. As the chapters progress, readers are guided through the evolving landscape of luxury, embracing themes of sustainability, digital innovation, and the intersection of opulence with responsibility. Arnault's cultural philanthropy takes center stage, showcasing his impact beyond business, fostering creativity, and contributing to global cultural enrichment. The chapters conclude with a forward-looking perspective, contemplating the future of luxury, ethical imperatives, and the unending story of visionaries shaping the industry. The legacy unveiled is not just a historical account but a call to future leaders and visionaries to continue crafting the narrative of opulence, responsibility, and cultural influence in the ever-evolving world of luxury.

www.ingramcontent.com/pod-product-compliance
Lightning Source LLC
LaVergne TN
LVHW010440070526
838199LV00066B/6105